The Family Connection Guide

Everything You Need to Know About Getting Ahead of a Stressful Family Situation

BETH HENRY

First published by Ultimate World Publishing 2023
Copyright © 2023 Beth Henry

ISBN

Paperback: 978-1-922982-66-7
Ebook: 978-1-922982-67-4

Beth Henry has asserted her rights under the Copyright, Designs and Patents Act 1988 to be identified as the author of this work. The information in this book is based on the author's experiences and opinions. The publisher specifically disclaims responsibility for any adverse consequences which may result from use of the information contained herein. Permission to use information has been sought by the author. Any breaches will be rectified in further editions of the book.

All rights reserved. No part of this publication may be reproduced, stored in or introduced into a retrieval system, or transmitted in any form, or by any means (electronic, mechanical, photocopying, recording or otherwise) without the prior written permission of the author. Any person who does any unauthorized act in relation to this publication may be liable to criminal prosecution and civil claims for damages. Enquiries should be made through the publisher.

Cover design: Ultimate World Publishing
Layout and typesetting: Ultimate World Publishing
Editor: Carmela Julian Valencia

Ultimate World Publishing
Diamond Creek,
Victoria Australia 3089
www.writeabook.com.au

Contents

Introduction 1

Chapter 1: The Needs for Basic Information 7

Chapter 2: Family Information for Everyone Involved 11

Chapter 3: Health Essentials 15

Chapter 4: Employment & Financial Management 19

Chapter 5: Property Knowledge 23

Chapter 6: Important Professional Contacts 29

Chapter 7: Power of Attorney & Wills 33

Chapter 8: Getting the Conversation Started … You've Got This! . . . 37

Afterword 41

Introduction

A phone call or text has left you speechless and in a daze. A family crisis has taken your breath away.

I've created this book specifically for those of you who would like to be better prepared for an *unexpected* emergency. I'm not speaking of the passing of a loved one. I'm referring to an emergency that requires your attention now—like Mom or Dad has had a fall or an allergic reaction to a new prescription. Or, more seriously, a heart attack or stroke.

The minute you hear the news, all the emotions, anxiety, panic, confusion come crashing in. You grab your keys, and out the door you go. While driving to them, your mind is racing with so many questions: How did this happen? What's been going on? I hope she's going to be OK. Who can I call to get the kids? I'll have to cancel my appointment tonight. Do I even have Mom's doctor's number?

A frantic search of your cell phone results in no luck with any contact information. And now you feel guilty; you should know this!

Maybe you have already experienced a situation like this. Do you remember the panic? Do you remember all the questions you were unsure of? Did you wish you were better prepared?

If this is you, keep reading, and I will show you how to do exactly that.

THE FAMILY CONNECTION GUIDE

According to a recent study, 47% of adults aged 40 to 59 have a parent aged 65+ and are raising a child or still supporting a young adult aged 18 or older!

– Pew Research Center

My name is Beth Henry. I'm a daughter, a sister, a wife, a mother and a grandmother. I'm in my late fifties, have a very busy life and wear many hats in my family, as I'm sure you do too. We always seem to be looking for that extra hour in the day. I'm also a real estate agent primarily assisting seniors looking at their options to either downsize their current home or stay and age in place.

Many of my clients have adult children who, for the most part, are very involved with their parents' day-to-day. However, many of us are not involved due to our busy schedules, careers, children, or the long distances to travel just to see them.

Sure, we know that Dad plays cards at the legion on Thursday nights and Mom volunteers at the animal shelter a few days a week. But many of us don't know when their last doctor's appointment was or if they are taking any type of medication besides the odd aspirin for an ache because they've been in the garden or garage too long.

If this sounds familiar, stay with me.

I thought about my parents. My dad had what we thought was a heart attack many years ago, and it turned out to be something I couldn't even pronounce. I don't think there were any complications from it. He looks great and travels south every winter. My mom takes something for her high blood pressure, but I couldn't tell you what the name of it is. I know they both have wills in place, but that's all I was aware of.

INTRODUCTION

I'd like to see them on a regular basis, but there's just not enough hours in the day some weeks. When we do get together, they want to know how I am; they don't want to talk about their problems.

Many of us have already dealt with a situation with our parents. But did you know, according to a recent poll from The Harris Poll,

"Only 33% of us know what to do and have a plan if our parents are required to stay in the hospital for any length of time!"

That would mean 67% of us don't! Admittedly, I was part of this group. We didn't have a plan. We never talked about what to do.

According to a Forbes article, 43% of parents haven't had detailed conversations with family members about long-term or elder care, and another 23% haven't had any conversations on these topics at all! So don't feel bad if you're part of this group. It's not your fault.

Many organizations and websites are available for a specific illness or end-of-life wishes and how to go about it. But what about today or tomorrow and the what-ifs and temporary issues or, as a client once said, "a bump in the road"? Would you know where to find the important documents? Could you temporarily pay their bills if they were unable to? And the stress that's involved with these tasks can be overwhelming. If you've been through this type of situation, you know exactly what I'm talking about.

Many of us are organized; we have to be to get through our very busy days. If we aren't, it can really blow up our schedules. But some of us haven't thought about a situation with our parents because we truly believe that it won't happen today or tomorrow or Saturday night as we just sit down to watch everything we have taped on our DVRs. I'm sure your parents have scheduled appointments six months from now. Do you know when they are or where they are?

There's so much to know, and as I started to think about it all, I began to worry. I could feel the stress building, and I wasn't in a crisis. There had to be a way to have that information at the ready even when I wasn't thinking clearly.

So, I began to research online. I found many websites, books and articles to read and some forms to fill out, print off and file away in a drawer. You know that drawer. We all have one. The catch-all drawer. The one we clean out once in a while because we can't put anything else in it!

Some of the articles I found were very informative. There were many books to read, but some were more than 200 pages. Who had time to read that? There had to be a better way.

In my research I also found many websites for help with our aging parents and the signs we should look for, but that can be difficult if you don't live close to your parents. Having been part of looking after my father-in-law as he dealt with his failing health, I understand how hard it can be on the family; we were a two-hour drive away. I wanted to get ahead of a crisis like that. I didn't want to go through that physical, mentally draining stress again. I needed to be better prepared; have the answers to the many questions that were to come for my mom and dad.

After spending countless hours going through the maze of websites and not finding what I was looking for, I decided to take matters into my own hands and created *The Family Connection Guide*.

It's short, simple and easy to read, including the fillable forms. Once those forms are completed, you'll not only have the medical information you will be looking for, you'll also have the answers to the legal and family tree information—right down to the mechanic or housekeeper who may have a spare key to their vehicle or home.

I have also created *The Family Connection Guide* e-book, allowing you to complete the forms from your cell or computer. I have found this is the easiest way to have that critical information when the walls are closing in, when you're

INTRODUCTION

in crisis mode. There's no need to print them off and file away in a drawer, never to be seen again.

You will have the answers to the many questions. You will have the contact info for the doctor, specialist and even the pharmacy they use and the medications they are taking, including the correct dosages or allergies they may have. I can't tell you how many stories I have been told about allergic reactions to patients because the emergency room team did not know about any. This is so important.

The Family Connection Guide will also help you stay organized with this vital information, as you can update them any time. You will have organized information readily available in one place. You will not have to go looking for it in crisis mode.

With e-mail capabilities from your cell, you will be able to e-mail or text this information to the hospital before you even arrive!

Can you imagine the looks on the faces and the relief in the voices of the emergency staff? You will feel so much better and less stressed knowing that you have this vital information at a moment's notice.

I understand that we are all very busy with our days, and that's the reason behind these pages. Let me show you how to get this done. It's not complicated. Rather, it is very simple. Doing it now will help lessen the stress you and your family will face during a crisis.

I have seen the unknown hold up many families in crisis at a time when they need to be with their parents instead of looking for documents to keep the lights on. It's like having a fire escape plan for the family. We all know we should have one, but because we have a smoke detector and know where the door is, too often we believe that everything will be OK.

I'm not saying you're going to have a fire; however, one day you will need to deal with your parents' health and need to have a plan, or at least a conversation, about how to deal with an *unexpected* emergency.

We can't afford not to be organized and have this key information today for those unexpected life events.

Begin the steps of having this crucial information in the palm of your hand. Start today! Make the time to give the best possible care you can before you and your family are in crisis mode.

This guide is intended to help you get ahead of a stressful family event.

Plan for *when*, not *if*.

We all seem to have a device in our hands.

Let's be responsible and have what really matters in them.

Chapter 1

The Needs for Basic Information

"Only 33% of us know what to do or have a plan if our parents are required to stay in the hospital for any length of time."

– The Harris Poll

Basic knowledge streamlines the emergency response. This form is very simple, and you can probably fill in all the blanks without much research.

It may seem odd to write down the date while completing this form, but doing so will help you remember when you entered the information. Hopefully, you will not need it for some time.

My advice is to have your parents at the table when filling in these forms, so they can see why you are asking the questions. Explain the benefits of having these questions answered now rather than in crisis mode, when everyone isn't thinking clearly.

Faith can be very important to some of our parents, so ask them if there is someone they would like you to contact if the need arises. Making such arrangements now can be very helpful.

I know what you're thinking. Why would they want to speak to someone of faith? They're not dying! Some of our parents feel better once they have spoken to their minister or pastor during difficult times. This may be one of those times.

I have included "Completed by" and "Witnessed by" on this form. This will go a long way with the lawyers and other professionals as to who has this information and when.

BASIC INFORMATION

Today's Date: _____

Given Name: _____

Birthdate: _____ Birth City/Province: _____

Birth Country: _____ Citizenship: _____

Social Insurance Number: _____

Health Card Number: _____

Drivers Licence Number: _____

E-mail Address: _____

Current Address/Residence: _____

City: _____ Province: _____ Postal Code: _____

Telephone #: _____ Cell #: _____

Military Service: _____

Religious Affiliation: _____

Contact Name: _____ Contact #: _____

Forms Completed by: _____ Date: _____

Relationship: _____

Witnessed by: _____ Date: _____

Relationship: _____

Chapter 2

Family Information for Everyone Involved

"43% of parents have not had detailed conversations with family members about long-term care & elder care; ... and another 23% haven't had any conversations on these topics at all!"

– Forbes article

This form is for everyone that will be involved. Hospitals like to have family tree information regarding who will likely be at the hospital during those non-visitation hours. It's not imperative that they have it, but the more information they have, the better. Having it helps everyone with the transition of care and with what information can be given out and to whom. Family dynamics, good and bad, will be ever present in a crisis situation.

This form asks for the spouse information. If your parent is single, just skip those lines. If they do have a spouse, this comes in handy. I had witnessed an elderly couple dealing with an emergency wherein the husband was admitted to the hospital due to fainting and the wife due to stress during that crisis situation. It is handy referencing your parents' information on each of their forms, as is having their children's and grandchildren's names and contact information.

Neighbours may be knowledgeable of the day-to-day routine at your parents' home. If this is the case, and with your parents' permission, include their contact information on this page. Doing so may well be beneficial for everyone, as they could be asked to help out by getting the mail or picking up the paper from the end of their driveway and keep an eye on the house while you are taking care of your parents.

I have also included what some may find a little odd—pets! Yes, pets. I believe they are part of the family, and in some cases, the only family close and living with your parents. They are very important and cannot be forgotten.

I know of a situation where the family only realized at the hospital that their beloved family dog was at home and had been since. So, make sure you involve their pets and have a plan for them too.

FAMILY INFORMATION

Single:____ Widowed:____ Divorced:____ Common-Law:____ Married:____

Marriage Date: _____ City of Marriage: _____

Name of Spouse: _____

Spouse Birthdate: _____ Birth City: _____

Spouse Health Card #: _____

Spouse Social Insurance #: _____

Spouse E-mail Address: _____

Military Service: _____

Residence Address: _____

City: _____ Province: _____ Postal Code: _____

Telephone #: _____ Cell #: _____

Religious Affiliation: _____

Contact Name: _____ Contact #: _____

Number of Children: _____ Number of Grandchildren: _____

Child Name: _____

Contact #: _____ E-mail: _____

Child Name: _____

Contact #: _____ E-mail: _____

Other Contact Name: _____

Contact #: _____ E-mail: _____

Pets: Yes ___ No ___ Names: _____

Veterinary: _____

Contact #: _____

Chapter 3

Health Essentials

More than 50% of adverse drug reaction-related hospital admissions are preventable.

– US National Library of Medicine

Along with the family tree information, the hospital will ask you many questions about your parents' day-to-day health. This form will give them vital information in an emergency. You may still have to fill out some forms specific to that hospital, but you will have the information at your fingertips, giving you more time with your parents.

This form has a lot of information to collect, but if I were to enter anything at all, it would be their primary family doctor's contact information. You can always update the form if their needs change.

In most cases, their doctor would have the other specialist, blood type and health insurance information, as they would have recommended the specialist and have had dealings with their insurance company. Meanwhile, having their pharmacist's contact information is the best way to gain knowledge of all medications, past and present. They may use a few different pharmacies, so please ask them.

Also, insurance questions can be very frustrating, period. If you don't have the necessary information, it may cause delays in getting the care your parents require. I'm sure there are many stories regarding care and insurance. *Please* take the time to obtain the correct information.

Some questions to consider:

- When was their last visit to the optometrist, if they require glasses? Funny story: I had a client whose husband had no idea that his wife required glasses until she was at the hospital for a procedure. She felt she didn't need them and didn't want to tell anyone, including her husband. Her last visit to the eye doctor was fifteen years previous!
- Do your parents have a home care service come in weekly? Monthly? They may have some insight into the day-to-day.
- Do they take any medication? If so, what are they taking, and what are the reasons behind the prescription? Allergic reactions to medications will be avoided if you have the correct information. You can enter this information on the Medical Details page of the form.

HEALTH INFORMATION

Family Doctor Name: _____

Tel#: _____ E-mail: _____

Pharmacy Info: _____ Tel#: _____

Specialist Name: _____

Tel#: _____ E-mail: _____

Dentist Name: _____

Tel#: _____ E-mail: _____

Eye Glasses? Yes ___ No ___ Optometrist Name: _____

Tel#: _____ E-mail: _____

Blood Type: _____ Organ Donor? Yes__ No__ Completed Forms: Yes __ No __

Hearing Aid: Yes__ No__ Artificial Limbs: Yes__ No__

Independent Health Insurance: Yes___ No___

Company: _____ Tel#: _____

Policy #: _____ Plan & Client ID #: _____

Home Care Service Company: _____

Case Worker Name: _____ Tel#: _____

List Health Concerns or challenges: *More space on next page*

_____

_____

_____

_____

MEDICAL DETAILS

For: _____

Medications   *Reason*   *Date started*

_____

_____

_____

_____

_____

_____

_____

_____

Surgeries: _____

_____

_____

_____

Allergies: _____

_____

_____

_____

Recent challenges or concerns: _____

_____

_____

_____

Chapter 4

Employment & Financial Management

I've included employment on this form, as it may or may not be a concern. If one or both of your parents are still at their full-time career or working part-time, you will need to let their employer know they will not be coming in due to the situation. Having their employment information will cut some of your legwork down.

Banking information is also crucial. If your parents are unable to take care of their finances for a period of time or not at all, you will need to have this in order before an emergency. Not having this organized can create many problems in a crisis situation. Doing this groundwork now will save so much time and stress for you and your parents.

Speak to your bank personnel and ask what needs to be done to avoid problems if the need arises for you to temporarily pay their bills. The banks are more than happy to help you and the family arrange a simple meeting. This will also lessen the legwork they need to do if their rules have not been met. Every bank has its own set of rules when it comes to privacy, so ask them.

Another challenge may be your parents feeling that you don't need to know any of their financial information; they will just shut down the conversation. They may not want you to know about their mortgage or line of credit. That's OK. Most parents don't discuss money, as their generation never spoke about it.

How much money our parents have or don't have is a delicate subject. Please don't just call them and say, "I need to know your bank account number!" That won't help anyone. Again, speak to your bank—they do this delicate dance almost every day.

Many parents have a credit card or two. If you have the banking in order, you can pay their credit card with their bank. However, some parents deal directly with the credit card company. If so, call the credit card company and ask what they need to have this done temporarily. Again, every company has different rules regarding privacy. (See Chapter 7 on Power of Attorney)

The pension program in the United States is similar to the Canada Pension Plan and covers most persons who work. However, to qualify for a benefit under most pension programs, you normally must have contributed to the program for a minimum period.

Your parents may be receiving other government benefits such as OAS (Old Age Security) Disability Benefits, SSDI (Social Security Disability Insurance) or LTD (Long Term Disability) Coverage from their employer. These benefits are usually referenced by their social security or social insurance numbers. If you require more space, you can enter the information on the last page, named "Additional Details."

Do your parents have an RRIF (Registered Retirement Income Fund) or RRSP (Registered Retirement Savings Plan)? They may have an independent pension from a former employer or a private life Insurance plan. You will need the plan and policy number along with a client identification number.

Ensure you have the correct information.

Please don't let this chapter stall you with your progress. It may be very stressful having a conversation with your parents regarding finances, and it may take some time for them to wrap their minds around the fact that you are asking for this information. Think about how you would feel if your kids started asking what bank you use and needed your account number.

Let your parents know it's not about the numbers or the amount of money they have. You just want to be able to temporarily keep their home and finances in order while they are recovering.

EMPLOYMENT & FINANCIAL INFORMATION

Employed: Yes___ No___ Self Employed____

Company Name: _____

Address: _____

Contact Tel #: _____ Manager: _____

Bank: _____

Address: _____

Telephone #: _____ Bank Manager: _____

Chequing Account #: _____

Savings Account #: _____

Line of Credit #: _____

Mortgage: Yes___ No___ Mortgage Acct #: _____

Mortgage Company: _____

Mortgage Contact #: _____

Credit Card #: _____

Credit Card #: _____

Safety Deposit Box: Yes___ No___ Key location: _____

CPP:___ OAS:___ Disability:___ Other: _____

RRSP/RRIF: Yes___ No___ Plan # _____

Individual Company Pension: Yes____ No____

Company: _____

Contact Name: _____ Telephone #: _____

Plan or Client ID #: _____

(If you need more space for details, please use the back pages)

Chapter 5

Property Knowledge

Entering your parents' address may seem a bit silly, as you have already entered it in the Basic Information. If you have *The Family Connection Guide* e-book, it should already be entered.

This form is self-explanatory, and you should know most of this information. But if you live in different towns, you may not know all of it. Have they downsized and are now renting the home they live in?

Our postal services in Canada have been changing, and some towns are no longer receiving mail at their doors. They are now delivering mail to a community superbox area. Do you know where that is?

Property insurance information is important too. Generally, a home is considered vacant after thirty days. Most typical home insurance policies won't provide full coverage for the property. It's worth a call to the insurance company to get the correct information on the policy.

Some parents are snowbirds and have property in the south where they winter. If they have a property management company looking after things, have that information in case the need arises.

Utility companies have their own rules and regulations. Each one is different. Our hydro (electric) company would not discuss anything with me, as my husband's name is the only name on the account. The only way they would speak to me was to add my name to the account. However, our gas company would give me all the information I asked for and let me set up a service call even without my name on the account. Meanwhile, our TV and phone service was a whole other game. They are now texting me with a one-time code to make sure it's me who is calling for information.

Technology is ever-changing. My advice is to give each utility company a call and see what their privacy requirements are. Again, you don't need to call anyone if you have the information at the ready and a plan with your parents as to what needs to be done and how it's to be done in crisis mode.

Many of our parents have a vehicle or two. They could also have pleasure vehicles, like boats and trailers and the like. Enter the VIN (Vehicle Identification Number) for each vehicle along with the insurance company contact information too. Doing so will make things a lot easier if you need to deal with a situation while your parents are unable to take care of things.

My parents had a fifty-foot boat. They loved it, but my dad was always doing something with it or calling someone else to maintain it. I didn't have a clue about any of the things that needed to be done with it.

Just like mine, your parents may have an item that has a lot of behind-the-scenes attached to maintaining it, if you know what I mean, so get the information on these items. It's all about *you* being less stressed in a crisis situation.

Other properties can include antiques, jewellery and family heirlooms. Most families know who will get the grandfather clock or the pearl necklace. A family emergency or even a temporary situation may bring out the family dynamics—the good, the bad and the ugly—so make sure that you have that conversation with your parents and make a plan to have a plan.

Our grandmother—Nana, as we called her—had masking tape on the back of everything (I mean everything), noting the name she wanted that certain item to go to. We all knew it; she told everyone. It wasn't perfect, but when we had to move her things out of the house, it made things a bit easier.

PROPERTY KNOWLEDGE

You can make an appointment with an estate lawyer. They typically only deal with estates and wills; however, they can be instrumental in helping you put this together. I have heard comments that people don't want to spend the money to get this done, so doing this can be the next best thing. You can enter the information on the last page, the Additional Details page, or create your own page or direction.

Another type of property your parents have is password-protected property. They don't actually own it, but they have a username and a password to particular websites. This can include e-mail, social media, financial products and sites from which they regularly purchase particular products.

We often forget about this kind of property, so ask them. They may not be comfortable giving you their passwords, but get them to let you know where they keep this information in case you need it later.

Most of us forget to save passwords and usernames; some apps can help us keep this information. This information has become a bigger part of our lives, and we need to treat them as important as we do our homes and vehicles.

PROPERTY INFORMATION

Home Address: _____

City: _____ Postal Code: _____

Own:___ Property Roll #: _____

Rent:___ Landlord Contact Info: _____

Mailbox Location (Street Name): _____ Box#: _____

Property Insurance Company: _____

Policy # _____ Contact Tel#: _____

Hydro/Electric Account: _____

Natural Gas/Propane Account: _____

Water Account: _____

Cellular Account: _____

Telephone Account: _____

2nd Home:___ Location: _____

Province/State: _____ Postal/Zip Code: _____

Management Company: _____

Vehicle: _____ VIN #: _____

Insurance Company: _____

Contact Tel #: _____ Policy #: _____

Vehicle: _____ VIN #: _____

Insurance Company: _____

Contact Tel#: _____ Policy#: _____

(If you need more space for details, please use the back pages)

Password Protected Property

Website   Username   Password

_____

_____

_____

_____

_____

_____

_____

_____

_____

_____

_____

_____

_____

_____

_____

(If you need more space for details, please use the back pages)

Chapter 6

Important Professional Contacts

This will be your go-to page, as it will include all of your parents' professional contact details. If your parents don't have a lawyer or accountant, you can help find one, or perhaps they can speak to the one you use or one their neighbours recommend.

Please ensure you have a conversation about lawyers and accountants and what they can do for them—especially while everyone is healthy and able. Many family conflicts can start if this is not done while the parents are healthy and well.

My mom and her husband did their own taxes. They didn't have an accountant. They always said they could do it and that hiring one was a waste of money. They knew how to do it, and there was no arguing with them on that one. Unfortunately, my mom's husband recently passed away. Now she has an accountant and a lawyer, as she isn't clear on everything that needs to be done or how to do it. He took care of all of that.

If your parents do have an accountant, get their or their company's contact information. Record the last time they visited too. If they do not have one, please find out if the previous year's taxes were done and sent to the government—this topic is a whole book in itself.

If your parents have already done their due diligence and have appointed POA (power of attorney), enter the names and contact information. If there is a last will and testament, make sure the location is noted. In many cases, their lawyer will also have a copy of the will.

Consent forms are not that popular any longer but are very important to individual companies if there is an individual authorized to act on the parents' behalf. They are probably unaware of the POA, if there is one, and will need that documentation. They may also require original documentation and not photocopies. If there are consent forms for particular companies, enter their names and contact information.

PROFESSIONAL INFORMATION

Lawyer: _____

Contact Info: _____

e-mail address: _____

Last visit: _____

Accountant: _____

Contact Info: _____

E-mail Address: _____

Last visit: _____

Documentation

Power of Attorney Medical: Yes _____   No _____

Name: _____ Contact #: _____

Power of Attorney Financial: Yes _____   No _____

Name: _____ Contact #: _____

Last Will & Testament: Yes___ No____   Birth Certificate: Yes____ No____

Location of Documentation: _____

Company Consent Form: _____

Contact Information: _____

Company Consent Form: _____

Contact Information: _____

Company Consent Form: _____

Contact Information: _____

Chapter 7

Power of Attorney & Wills

Power of Attorney: A power of attorney (POA) is a legal document that gives one party the legal authority to act on another's behalf to manage legal and financial affairs. The power can be very broad to allow complete control over all finances and property, or it can be limited to a specific task.

As there are many types of POA, please seek legal advice on what's best for your family situation.

Will: A will or testament is a legal document that expresses a person's wishes as to how their property will be distributed after their death and which person will manage the property until its final distribution.

Please understand the laws where you live. Each state, province or country has its own laws relating to a power of attorney and a will.

We don't like to talk about this subject for some reason, but everyone has thought about a will. Should I have one? Should I write something down? Should I ask someone to make decisions for me if I can't?

YES, YES and YES!

We should all have a will. However, the majority of us do not have a legal will. The word *legal* is questionable too. How does one know what a "legal will" is?

I could make this chapter a hundred pages or more, but the reason for this guide is to give you simple and easy answers. And the best answer I can give you is to do some research. Be careful when searching online, however. Call a lawyer and ask if they could help you organize one. Ask questions and ask again if you don't understand the answer given.

I know that the government doesn't care if you have one or not and can hold things up for you and your family if things are not organized, as per the laws where you live.

There will be many factors and misunderstandings when there is no will in place. For instance, I've had conversations with friends who believe that if they were to suddenly pass away, their spouse would get everything they left behind. But, depending on where you live, that could be the farthest from the truth. Your estate may not go to your spouse but to other family members. There are so many different scenarios, and the laws where you live dictate how your estate will be distributed.

I know of an instance wherein the husband did not receive his wife's estate—everything they had saved and worked for. Her parents did, as they were her next of kin.

This will ultimately create difficulties for families trying to deal with the death of their loved one and now have to deal with uncertainty and confusion regarding what would happen to the estate after.

Some think they don't have anything to leave, so why bother? Many think, *I don't own a house or a car; I'm still living at home with my parents. I don't need a will.*

But if you are a legal adult (in most states and countries, that would be 18 years old), you will need a last will and testament. There are many types of wills, from the basic to the more detailed. You need to research and speak to a lawyer who knows the laws where you live.

POWER OF ATTORNEY & WILLS

I am not an expert on this topic, so you need to take the steps and speak with a lawyer. Lawyers are professionals and deal with the specifics involved every day. Don't make the mistake of trying to understand the ins and outs of this legal creature on your own—it can and will take on a life of its own, believe me!

Most lawyers will give a free 30-minute consultation, either on the phone, on Zoom or in person, to help you understand what type of will you need. Laws are constantly changing, and lawyers are up-to-date with them all. That's what they do. So, do the family a favour, and start taking the steps and see a lawyer.

Some may disagree with me, but at least do some research. Read some stories about what a family has gone through when a loved one passed without a will. Some communities have free nights with a lawyer to help understand the paperwork involved. Be careful about merely believing what you see online or hear through the grapevine. Each province, state and country have different compliance laws.

No matter their lifestyle, it is important to discuss this with your parents. Again, the numbers are not important here. Have the conversation. As aging adults ourselves, we need to have this information organized for our own benefit, if not theirs. Doing so will make things so much more manageable.

Chapter 8

Getting the Conversation Started ... You've Got This!

Starting the conversation can be an overwhelming task for many of us.

How do I talk to my parents about this?

Will they think that I think they are dying? Will they think I'm being nosey?

Do they think I just want to know how much money they have?

They'll think I just want to know who will get what and how much I get.

These are the thoughts that linger while we think about the daunting talk. I'll be honest, I didn't have a clue on how to go about it, but I knew I had to figure it out. I had to be better prepared.

I got a phone call from my mom one day, telling me she had her cataracts done and could see so much better! I was a little taken aback by her comment; I didn't even know she was having any issues with her eyes.

I remember getting another phone call from my mom one morning to let me know that my stepfather had a diabetic attack and had been rushed to the hospital the night before. I drove to their house, angry that I hadn't known he had any attacks at all! Why hadn't she told me? I could have helped her out. By the time I got to her, I had calmed down, but I did ask her later why she hadn't told me about his attacks. Her response was that I was too busy, and she didn't want to bother me.

It's been a while since those events occurred, and my stepfather has since passed away. Mom says she's doing better. She's also more talkative with me and shares her day's events. We have talked about her will and where her important documents are, including what she would like to happen after she leaves this world.

I know there are things I don't know, and that's OK. I don't need to know everything. It's not my business, and she's over eighteen. As she would say, "Last time I looked, I didn't need your permission to do anything!"

I tell you these stories to point out that some families are very aware, or think they are, of their parents' day-to-day and that some parents don't want to bother their adult children because they know they are busy with their own families or don't want them to know and start to worry.

As an adult, I do things a little differently than my parents. To me, I seem a little more detailed or a bit more "on top of things" with certain events. Some of our parents are a little bit more lax on things. I hear the saying from my parents and clients of that generation all the time, "It'll do" or "Don't worry about it; I'll manage."

As for starting the conversation, you know your parents and how they will respond to these kinds of questions. Some folks have told me to start the conversation while the whole family is together in a casual setting, such as a family BBQ. But, depending on your family, that may not be the right time. Dad might not want to talk about anything while Uncle Larry is around, if you know what I mean.

Perhaps your parents are telling you a story about one of their neighbours and the challenges they are dealing with in a crisis situation. This could offer an opportunity to begin a discussion and ask if they have a plan. You might not get any answers that day, but you have opened up at least one more occasion to discuss and have the conversation. Let them mull it over; ponder what you have just asked them. Give them time. They may have thought about things but just haven't gotten to it.

GETTING THE CONVERSATION STARTED ... YOU'VE GOT THIS!

Why do so many people fail to tackle or complete estate planning? The top two reasons of the people surveyed: 47% haven't gotten around to it!

– AARP

Regardless of how you arrive at having the conversation, don't go to their house with guns a-blazing, demanding answers as to where or what they have gotten in place. That will shut down the conversation. Period!

I remember my stepmother calling to ask me to be the executor of their estate more than thirty years ago. I was a little taken aback by the question. They are very organized and always have things in place. I just wasn't ready for the conversation, but so glad that she called to let me know they were putting things in place. She even told me the location of their important documents. At the time, I didn't realize the importance of the phone call.

When the discussion begins, assure your parents that you don't need to know anything about money. That's not the reason you are having the conversation; you just need to be prepared for an emergency when it happens. If other family members are present, don't talk about them like they're not in the room; that will get you nowhere fast! Let them know that having the information will lessen the stress that will creep into your lives while in crisis mode.

I believe that there are three major subjects that need to be addressed when having this discussion:

- **Health:** Get a list of any medications or allergies as well as their doctors' or specialist's contact info.
- **Professional Contacts:** Their lawyer's and accountant's, if any.
- **Finances:** Regarding their banking details, have a discussion with their bank officials on what is needed to be done if there is an emergency.

Another important topic to discuss is who the leader, caregiver and go-to person will be if there is an emergency. Have this in place; I can't stress this enough. I have been involved with family members who wanted to be in control of it all while in crisis mode but got angry because they were doing it all. Like I said, chaos and stress creep into your lives without even realizing it.

You are the only one who knows where you need to begin. If you haven't thought about any of this, that's great! It means you haven't had a crisis or an emergency that immediately required your attention.

Afterword

There are many statistics out there, but here are a few from Harris Poll that I find very interesting:

Only 16% of adults 65+ have done a financial inventory of accounts and shared paperwork with family members or trusted representatives.

Only 29% have ensured that proper paperwork is in place.

Only 33% have communicated with their family members or trusted representatives about their wishes, should they become incapacitated.

I have read many articles on how to begin a conversation with parents and what to do in a crisis situation as a daughter, and what I have learned through my experience as a real estate agent. I hope I have given you some ideas on how to start the conversation.

Each of us will have to deal with a situation sooner or later with our parents, so I do hope you will take the time to start completing these forms before your family is in a crisis. It may take a day or two, or longer if needed, depending on your parents' willingness to have this information at the ready.

Whatever you decide, feel good about getting organized and having a plan in place. You can also just give this guide to your parents and have them complete it but let you know where they keep it.

Today is the best day to start!

It's always too early to talk about it ... until it's too late!

Good luck and all the very best to you and your family.

Beth

www.thefamilyconnectionguide.com

e-mail: beth@thefamilyconnectionguide.com

Additional Details

Use this page for other important information or if you need additional space;
(e.g.: Mechanic, Housekeeper, Landscaping etc.)

Additional Details

Use this page for other important information or if you need additional space;
(e.g.: Mechanic, Housekeeper, Landscaping etc.)

Additional Details

Use this page for other important information or if you need additional space;
(e.g.: Mechanic, Housekeeper, Landscaping etc.)

Additional Details

Use this page for other important information or if you need additional space;
(e.g.: Mechanic, Housekeeper, Landscaping etc.)

_____

_____

_____

_____

_____

_____

_____

_____

_____

_____

_____

_____

_____

_____

_____

_____

Additional Details

Use this page for other important information or if you need additional space;
(e.g.: Mechanic, Housekeeper, Landscaping etc.)

Additional Details

Use this page for other important information or if you need additional space;
(e.g.: Mechanic, Housekeeper, Landscaping etc.)

Additional Details

Use this page for other important information or if you need additional space;
(e.g.: Mechanic, Housekeeper, Landscaping etc.)

Additional Details

Use this page for other important information or if you need additional space;
(e.g.: Mechanic, Housekeeper, Landscaping etc.)

Additional Details

Use this page for other important information or if you need additional space;
(e.g.: Mechanic, Housekeeper, Landscaping etc.)

www.ingramcontent.com/pod-product-compliance
Lightning Source LLC
Chambersburg PA
CBHW051320110526
44590CB00031B/4414